P9-DEL-643

Dedication

This book is dedicated to teachers ... those who influence our children each day, especially those who feel forgotten, unappreciated or under supported. You are the candle in the eyes of a troubled child—one who is lost, but whose "light for learning" has gone on because you have found him or her.

So, it is with the utmost pleasure that we dedicate this book to the millions of teachers who keep the candle burning in their students until the light turns on.

Never lose your passion for educating your students, for they become the leaders of tomorrow!

To our children and our grandchildren, remember that education is the key to success and to finding your way through life. Embrace your learning experience for it will be part of your life's journey as it has been part of ours.

Jack & Linda Podojil

Copyright © 2011 by Simple Truths, LLC

Published by Simple Truths, LLC
1952 McDowell Road, Suite 300
Naperville, Illinois 60563
800-900-3427

All rights reserved. No portion of this book may be reproduced,
stored in a retrieval system or transmitted in any form by any
means—except for brief quotations in printed reviews—
without the prior written permission of the publisher.

Simple Truths is a registered trademark.

Design: Simple Truths, Brian Frantz

Printed and bound in the United States of America

ISBN 978-1-60810-148-1

01 WOZ 11

To my greatest teacher and love,
you taught me much.
This is our book together.

Introduction

Among all the influences that have helped to shape my life, two stand out—teachers and quotations.

I grew up in Trenton, Tennessee, a small town of 5,000 people. I have wonderful memories of those first 18 years. And during those years, there were two teachers who I can say, with certainty, helped to make me who I am today. The first was Ms. Bridges, who taught me in the 4th grade. She was amazing! I'll never forget her beautiful smile and her passion for teaching. She made learning so much fun and made all of us feel as though we could do anything we wanted to do. The positive seeds she planted in my head are still growing!

Then there was Fred Culp, my history teacher in high school. To this day he is still the funniest person I've ever met. In addition to loving his history class, he taught me that a sense of humor, especially laughing at yourself, can be one of life's greatest blessings. He also, more than any teacher I ever had, made learning so much fun. His class was always the highlight of my day.

As most of you know, I also love quotations. That's why this book of inspirational quotes for teachers is so special to me. It's also made special by the two people who compiled these quotes—John and Linda Podojil.

In elementary school, John was hard of hearing and failed the first grade because only he knew he could not hear. He read people's lips to try and learn, but could not when they turned away from him. John was diagnosed with an 80 percent hearing loss and underwent an operation to restore his hearing. He was also a high school drop-out and it took special teachers to ignite his love of learning…so much so that he not only received a GED but an associate's degree as well.

John went on to teach technical education at the University of California San Diego, California State University Dominguez Hills and the College of Southern Nevada. He has presented at both Cornell University and Stanford, educated over 3,000 technical education instructors on safety in technical skills classrooms and is an advocate for technical education. John says his greatest teacher of all times is his wife, Linda.

Linda also was a teacher. Before retiring from the Boeing Company as full-time safety administrator at Boeing Portland and also in Seattle, Linda was a part-time safety instructor for South Seattle Community College, where she taught occupational safety and health related subjects.

John and Linda know that teachers who believe they can make a difference do make a difference.

In thanks for all the teachers who help to mold the next generation, enjoy *Inspirational Quotes for Teachers*.

Mac Anderson
Founder, Simple Truths

I touch the future. *I teach.*

Christa McAuliffe

———

*T*eaching is
the greatest act of optimism.

Colleen Wilcox

Who dares to teach must never cease to learn.

John C. Dana

The greatest gift

that you can give to another is
knowledge for knowledge is power—
power to build and to dream.
What you can envision in
your mind you can achieve.

Jack Podojil

The mediocre teacher tells.

The good teacher explains.

The superior teacher demonstrates.

The great teacher inspires.

William Arthur Ward

*Every truth
has four corners:*

as a teacher

*I give you one corner,
and it is for you
to find the other three.*

Confucius

$\mathcal{E}$ach second we live is a new and unique moment of the universe, a moment that will never be again. And what do we teach our children in school? We teach them that two and two make four, and that Paris is the capital of France. When will we also teach them what they are? We should say to each of them: Do you know what you are? You are a marvel. You are unique. In all the years that have passed, there has never been another child like you. Your legs, your arms, your cunning fingers, the way you move! You may be a Shakespeare, a Michelangelo, a Beethoven. You have the capacity for anything. Yes, you are a marvel. And when you grow up, can you then harm another who is, like you, a marvel? You must work, we must all work, to make the world *worthy of its children.*

Pablo Picasso

Teaching is not a profession; it's a passion.
Without your passion and dedication,
our children's future would resemble a sunset
instead of a sunrise. Your days are long and
often difficult. Thrive on your passion,
and enhance our world's tomorrow.

Linda A. Podojil

A teacher affects eternity;

he can never tell where his influence stops.

Henry Adams

Tell me and I forget.
Teach me and I remember.
Involve me and I learn.

Benjamin Franklin

The greatest sign of a success for a teacher…

is to be able to say,

"The children are now working

as if I did not exist."

Maria Montessori

I am a teacher.

It is the greatest gift that life could give me,

since I am allowed to spend my days with

the future of the world. My students will be

presidents, doctors, lawyers, and craftspersons,

but hopefully they will all be teachers to someone.

Jack Podojil

True teachers are those who use themselves as bridges over which they invite their students to cross, then having facilitated their crossing, joyfully collapse, encouraging them to create bridges of their own.

Nikos Kazantzakis

Good teachers know how to bring out the best in students.

Charles Kuralt

*M*ost of us end
up with no more than five
or six people who remember us.
Teachers have thousands of people
who remember them for
the rest of their lives.

Andy Rooney

In teaching you cannot see the fruit of a day's work.

It is invisible and remains so,
maybe for twenty years.

Jacques Barzun

*Teaching is not a profession;
it's a passion. Without passion for your
subject and a desire for your students
to learn and be the best in the world,
then we have failed as teachers
and failure is not an option.*

John F. Podojil

To teach is to learn twice.

Joseph Joubert

---

*The secret in education
lies in respecting the pupil.*

Ralph Waldo Emerson

The task of the excellent teacher is to stimulate "apparently ordinary" people to unusual effort. The tough problem is not in identifying winners:

it is in making winners out of ordinary people.

K. Patricia Cross

A teacher
Takes a hand
Opens a mind
Touches a heart
Shapes the future.

Author Unknown

The man who can make hard things easy
is the educator.

Ralph Waldo Emerson

Inspired teachers...

cannot be ordered by the gross

from the factory. They must be discovered

one by one, and brought home

from the woods and swamps like orchids.

They must be placed in a conservatory,

not in a carpenter shop;

and they must be honored and trusted.

John Jay Chapman

A good teacher is one who can **understand** *those who are not very good at explaining, and* **explain** *to those who are not very good at understanding.*

Dwight D. Eisenhower

 have a present

that is challenging, adventurous and fun.

I am allowed to spend my days

with the future of our country, protecting the safety

and health of children in our schools.

Only those who dare to fail greatly,
can ever achieve greatly.

Jack Podojil

Teachers are expected to reach

unattainable goals

with inadequate tools.

The miracle is that at times

they accomplish this impossible task.

Haim Ginott

Do not train a child
to learn by force or harshness;
but direct them to it
by what amuses their minds,
so that you may be better able to discover,
with accuracy, the peculiar bent
of the genius of each.

Plato

*Education is much more
than a matter of imparting
the knowledge and skills by which narrow
goals are achieved.
It is also about opening the child's eyes to
the needs and rights of others.*

the Dalai Lama

The mark of
a well educated person is not
necessarily in knowing
all the answers, but in knowing
where to find them.

Douglas Everett

Education is the most powerful weapon which you can use to change the world.

Nelson Mandela

The dream begins with a teacher who believes in you, who tugs and pushes and leads you to the next plateau, sometimes poking you with a sharp stick called "truth."

Dan Rather

I don't divide the world into the weak and the strong, or the successes and the failures, those who make it or those who don't. I divide the world into learners and non-learners.

Benjamin R. Barber

Teachers must have passion about their subject to be able to teach it well.

Jack Podojil

A child miseducated is a child lost.

John F. Kennedy

He who is afraid of asking is ashamed of learning.

Danish Proverb

It is noble to teach oneself, but
still nobler to teach others
and less trouble.

Mark Twain

———

The most important part of teaching
is to teach what it is to know.

Simone Weil

The day someone quits school he is condemning himself to a future of poverty.

Jaime Escalante

Learn as though you would never be able to master it; hold it as though you would be in fear of losing it.

Confucius

Let us think of education

as the means of developing our greatest abilities,

because in each of us there is a private hope and

dream which, fulfilled, can be translated into

benefit for everyone and

greater strength for our nation.

John F. Kennedy

$\mathcal{I}$am a Special Education Teacher and I had the pleasure of having an autistic child in my classroom this year. Patric was a fifth grader and this June, when he was promoted to the sixth grade, he surprised me with a gift which he was eager for me to open. After opening the present and seeing that it was a beautiful table clock, Patric quickly asked if I knew why he had gotten me a clock.

I replied that I didn't and to that he most lovingly answered:

"Because every time
you look at the clock
you'll know
I love you all the time."

Gabriela Allardo

Upon the subject of education, not presuming to dictate any plan or system respecting it, I can only say that I view it as the most important subject which we as people can be engaged in.

Abraham Lincoln

You must have passion in your heart and knowledge in the subject to be able to teach it to someone else.

Jack Podojil

I cannot teach anybody anything;
I can only make them think.

Socrates

———

The highest result of education
is tolerance.

Helen Keller

Anyone who stops learning is old,

whether at twenty or eighty.

Anyone who keeps learning stays young.

The greatest thing in life

is to keep your mind young.

Henry Ford

We teach best that which
we most need to learn.

Richard Bach

The object of teaching a child
is to enable him to get along
without his teacher.

Elbert Hubbard

A GREAT TEACHER WILL:

Teach

with all his heart,

Teach

with full of love and joy,

Always

gives faith and hope to his students,

Always

believes that his students will perform their best,

And never

gives up teaching until his students receive awards!

Karen John

Seek education rather than grades.

Seek your best rather than someone else's.

Seek friendship rather than acceptance.

Seek worth rather than rank.

Seek to build rather than to tear down.

Seek laughter and love in spite of pain

and you will have learned to live.

Jaqui Sheehan

I tell my students
"You will achieve
the level of knowledge,
that you demonstrate
you want to achieve."

Jack Podojil

Teaching is leaving a vestige of oneself in the development of another. And surely the student is a bank where you can deposit your most precious treasures.

Eugene P. Bertin

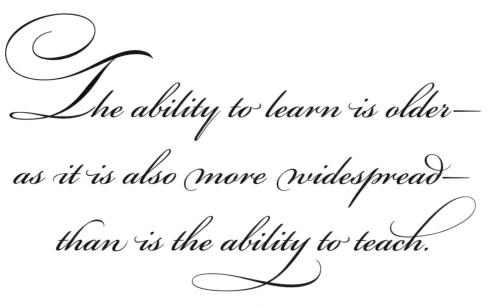

The ability to learn is older—
as it is also more widespread—
than is the ability to teach.

Margaret Mead

*Most teachers
are knowledgeable.
Good teachers are intelligent.
Great teachers are patient.
Exceptional teachers are
students themselves.*

Dale Dubin, M.D.

Children have real understanding only of that which they invent themselves, and each time that we try to teach them too quickly, we keep them from reinventing it themselves.

Jean Piaget

One looks back with appreciation to the brilliant teachers, but with gratitude to those who touched our human feelings. The curriculum is so much necessary raw material, but warmth is the vital element for the growing plant and for the soul of the child.

Carl Jung

*Whoso neglects
learning in his youth,
loses the past and
is dead for the future.*

Euripides

Teachers must regard every imperfection in the pupil's comprehension not as a defect but as a deficit in his or her own instruction, and endeavor to develop the ability to discover a new method of teaching.

Leo Tolstoy

I am a coach.

It is the greatest gift that life could give me,

since I am allowed to spend my days with the

future athletes of the world. My students will

be the best that I can teach them to be. I will

use my knowledge in the field of sports to

achieve these goals.

Jack Podojil

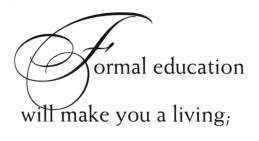ormal education
will make you a living;

self-education will make you a fortune.

Jim Rohn

Acquire new knowledge whilst thinking over

the old, and you may become a teacher of others.

Confucius

It's okay to make mistakes.

Mistakes are our teachers—

they help us to learn.

John Bradshaw

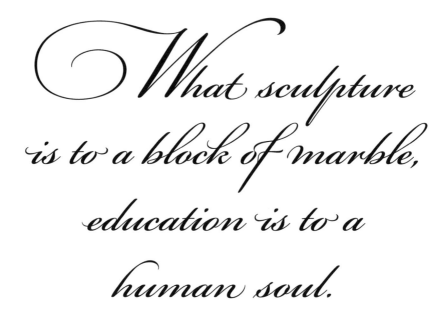

What sculpture is to a block of marble, education is to a human soul.

Joseph Addison

We should never pretend to know what we don't know, we should not feel ashamed to ask and learn from people below, and we should listen carefully to the views of the cadres at the lowest levels. Be a pupil before you become a teacher; learn from the cadres at the lower levels before you issue orders.

Mao Tse-tung

$\mathcal{E}$very child must be encouraged to get as much education as he has the ability to take. We want this not only for his sake—but for the nation's sake. Nothing matters more to the future of our country; not military preparedness—for armed might is worthless if we lack the brain power to build a world of peace; not our productive economy—for we cannot sustain growth without trained manpower; not our democratic system of government—for freedom is fragile if citizens are ignorant.

Lyndon B. Johnson

There are two educations.
One should teach us how
to make a living and the
other how to live.

John Adams

What we want

is to see the child in pursuit

of knowledge, and not knowledge

in pursuit of the child.

George Bernard Shaw

The world's future rests with technical education instructors educating the future craftspeople and professionals of tomorrow.

Jack Podojil

Teachers who educate children

deserve more honor than parents

who merely gave birth.

For bare life is furnished by the one,

the other ensures a good life.

Aristotle

*A*n education isn't how much you

have committed to memory, or even how

much you know. It's being able to differentiate

between what you do know and what you don't.

Anatole France

Education

is what remains after one

has forgotten what one

has learned in school.

Albert Einstein

They may forget what you said

but they will never forget

how you made them feel.

Carl Buechner

If your plan is for 1 year,

plant rice;

If your plan is for 10 years,

plant trees;

If your plan is for 100 years,

educate children.

Confucius

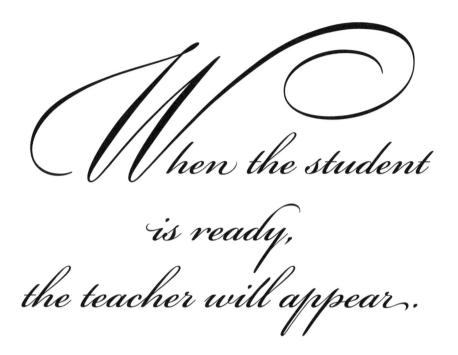

When the student
is ready,
the teacher will appear.

Buddhist Proverb

Education is an important element in the

struggle for human rights.

It is the means to help our children and

people rediscover their identity and

thereby increase self-respect.

Education is our passport to the future, for

tomorrow belongs to the people

who prepare for it today.

Malcolm X

Children are the messages we will send to a time we will never see.

Neil Postman

The business of teaching is carried forward...because some individuals of extraordinary vitality and strength of personality engage in it and the fire that helps to guide them kindles the spirits of the young people whose lives they touch.

Woodrow Wilson

The philosophy of the school room in one generation will be the philosophy of government in the next.

Abraham Lincoln

Education would be much more effective if its purpose was to ensure that by the time they leave school every boy and girl should know how much they do not know, and be imbued with a lifelong desire to know it.

Sir William Haley

In every school classroom, a student should be able to look around and see a model classroom where there are no safety or health hazards and where skilled instructors are protecting their safety and health by teaching them a professional skill on safe equipment in a safe and healthful environment.

Jack Podojil

77

We now accept the fact that learning is a lifelong process of keeping abreast of change. And the most pressing task is to teach people how to learn.

Peter F. Drucker

A teacher is one who makes himself progressively unnecessary.

Thomas Carruthers

Perhaps the most valuable result of all education is the ability to make yourself do the thing you have to do, when it ought to be done, whether you like it or not. It is the first lesson that ought to be learned; and however early a man's training begins, it is probably the last lesson that he learns thoroughly.

Thomas H. Huxley

The most extraordinary thing about a really good teacher is that he or she transcends accepted educational methods. Such methods are designed to help average teachers approximate the performance of good teachers.

Margaret Mead

You cannot teach
a man anything;
you can only help him find it
within himself.

Galileo

Good teachers are costly.

Bad teachers cost more.

Bob Talbert

*I'm not a teacher,
but an awakener.*

Robert Frost

---

*N*ine tenths of education
is encouragement.

Anatole France

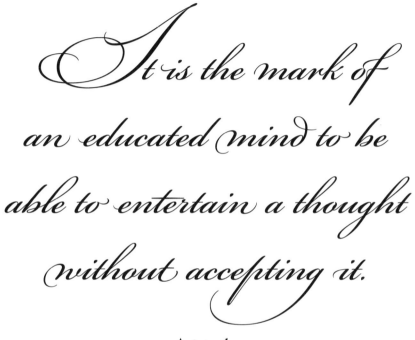

It is the mark of an educated mind to be able to entertain a thought without accepting it.

Aristotle

Education is the power to think clearly, the power to act well in the world's work, and the power to appreciate life.

Brigham Young

... Without books the development of civilization would have been impossible. They are the engines of change, windows of the world, lighthouses erected in the sea of time. They are companions, teachers, magicians, bankers of the treasures of the mind. Books are humanity in print.

Arthur Schopenhauer

Who dares to teach must never cease to learn.

John Cotton Dana

Education is the leading

of human souls to what is best,

and making what is best

out of them.

John Ruskin

You can't teach people everything they need to know. The best you can do is position them where they can find what they need to know when they need to know it.

Seymour Papert

The aim of education

should be to teach us rather how to think, than

what to think, rather to improve

our minds, so as to enable us

to think for ourselves,

than to load the memory

with the thoughts of other men.

John Dewey

Cultivate your garden.

Do not depend upon teachers to

educate you ... follow your own bent,

pursue your curiosity bravely, express

yourself, make your own harmony.

Will Durant

One of the beauties of teaching is that there is no limit to one's growth as a teacher, just as there is no knowing beforehand how much your students can learn.

Herbert Kohl

A child must learn early to believe that she is somebody worthwhile, and that she can do many praiseworthy things.

Benjamin Mays

No one has yet realized the wealth of sympathy, the kindness and generosity hidden in the soul of a child. The effort of every true education should be to unlock that treasure.

Emma Goldman

All of the top achievers
I know are lifelong learners ...
looking for new skills, insights,
and ideas. If they're not learning,
they're not growing ... not moving
toward excellence.

Denis Waitley

Creative activity could be described as a type of learning process where teacher and pupil are located in the same individual.

Arthur Koestler

Give the pupils something to do, not something to learn; and the doing is of such a nature as to demand thinking; learning naturally results.

John Dewey

The teacher who is indeed wise does not bid you to enter the house of his wisdom but rather leads you to the threshold of your mind.

Kahlil Gibran

Our greatest natural resource is
the minds of our children.

Walt Disney

Effective teaching may be
the hardest job there is.

William Glasser

What we become depends on what we read after all the professors have finished with us. The greatest university of all is a collection of books.

Thomas Carlyle

Instruction does much, but encouragement does everything.

Johann Wolfgang Von Goethe

You can teach a student a lesson for a day; but if you can teach him to learn by creating curiosity, he will continue the learning process as long as he lives.

Clay P. Bedford

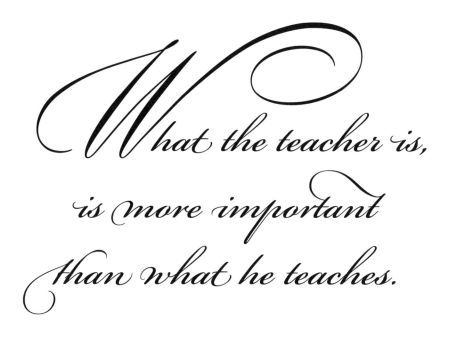

What the teacher is,
is more important
than what he teaches.

Karl A. Menninger

Education can be defined as working with people, young and old, to prepare them to live in the future. The future may be bright. The future may be gray. But, most importantly we must insure that there will be a future.

Willard J. Jacobson

A good teacher is one who helps you become who you feel yourself to be. A good teacher is also one who says something that you won't understand until 10 years later.

Julius Lester

In seeking wisdom, the first step is silence, the second listening, the third remembering, the fourth practicing, the fifth—teaching others.

Ibn Gabirol

Every child's life is like a piece of paper on which every person leaves a mark.

Chinese Proverb

What nobler employment,
or more valuable to the state,
than that of the man who instructs
the rising generation?

Marcus Tullius Cicero

To me, education is a leading out of what is already there in the pupil's soul.

Muriel Spark

What office is there which involves more *responsibility*, which requires more *qualifications*, and which ought, therefore, to be more *honorable*, than that of teaching?

Harriet Martineau

He that teaches us anything
which we knew not
before is undoubtedly to be
reverenced as a master.

Samuel Johnson

The good life is inspired by love and guided by knowledge.

Bertrand Russell

America's future will be determined by the home and the school. The child becomes largely what he is taught; hence we must watch what we teach, and how we live.

Jane Addams

It was a high counsel that I once heard given to a young person, "Always do what you are afraid to do."

Ralph Waldo Emerson

*J*ust remember the world is not a playground but a schoolroom.

Life is not a holiday but an education.

One eternal lesson for us all:

to teach us how better we should love.

Barbara Jordan

Education

is a progressive discovery

of our own ignorance.

Will Durant

*The secret in education
lies in respecting the pupil.*

Ralph Waldo Emerson

That's the point.

It goes like this:

Teaching is touching life.

Jaime Escalante

If a man empties his purse into his head, no man can take it away from him. An investment in knowledge always pays the best interest.

Benjamin Franklin

Give a man a fish and you feed him for a day. Teach a man to fish and you feed him for a lifetime.

Proverb

All of us

have two educations—

one which we receive from others;

another, and the most valuable,

which we give ourselves.

John Randolph

The faster you go,

the more students you leave behind. It doesn't

matter how much or how fast you teach. The

true measure is how much students have learned.

William Glasser

A student never forgets an encouraging private word, when it is given with sincere respect and admiration.

William Lyon Phelps

I always tell my students,
"Engage your brain before you engage
your mouth before you say anything since
your brain is the smarter of the two and
is usually right the first time.
If you say something before you think about it,
you may be wrong."

Jack Podojil

About the Authors

John Podojil

John's childhood hearing impairment did not impair his success in life. After surgery restored his hearing, he went on to obtain his GED and a college degree, later teaching technical education at the University of California San Diego, California State University Dominguez Hills and the College of Southern Nevada. John has presented at both Cornell University and Stanford University and has educated over 3,000 technical education instructors on safety in technical skills classrooms. An advocate for technical education, John has been honored as a catalyst to make the industrial workplace and Industrial Technology Education (TECH-ED) classrooms a safer environment for working and learning.

He is listed as an Honored Professional in the National Registry of Who's Who in America and currently writes safety articles for several national magazines. A member of the National Speakers Association, John is a requested motivational speaker at professional development conferences. He is also owner of Podojil & Associates, a private full-service safety, health, environmental and engineering consulting firm.

John can be reached at www.podojilconsulting.com

$\mathcal{L}$inda Podojil

Before retiring from the Boeing Company as full-time safety administrator at Boeing Portland and also in Seattle, Linda was a part-time faculty instructor for South Seattle Community College, where she taught occupational safety and health related subjects.

Linda has also been honored by the Minnesota Technology & Engineering Educators Association (MTEA) for her quest to make the industrial workplace and Industrial Technology Education (TECH-ED) classrooms a safer environment for working and learning.

An author who writes for national magazines, Linda has co-authored other motivational and educational books including Linda and John's latest book, *Teachers Pride: Everything You Would Like To Know About Popcorn and More*, Linda believes that to be a great teacher you must have passion. Her quote exhibits that, "Teaching is not a profession; it's a passion. Without your passion and dedication, our children's future would resemble a sunset instead of a sunrise. Your days are long and often difficult. Thrive on your passion, and enhance our world's tomorrow."

She and John live in Maricopa, Arizona. They have five children and eight grandchildren.

The simple truths® DIFFERENCE

If you have enjoyed this book we invite you to check out our entire collection of gift books, with free inspirational movies, at **www.simpletruths.com.** You'll discover it's a great way to inspire **friends** and **family,** or to thank your best **customers** and **employees.**

For more information, please visit us at:

www.simpletruths.com
Or call us toll free... **800-900-3427**